# GET A F*CK!NG JOB!

TEXT BY ELISE HOFFMANN AND CHRIS NIEMCZEWSKI
PHOTOGRAPHS BY ANTON PAPICH AND JEFF PREHN

NEW YORK

EDITED BY KAITLIN PUCCIO

GRAPHIC DESIGN BY JEFF SUTHERLAND

TEXT AND ARTWORK COPYRIGHT © 2018 ELISE HOFFMANN
ALL RIGHTS RESERVED
LIBRARY OF CONGRESS CONTROL NUMBER: 2017964146

WWW.BENTFRAMEPUBLISHING.COM

TO ALEX, SAM, MARTIN, AND JAKE

WE'RE HAPPY YOU'RE DONE WITH SCHOOL,
WE LOVE YOUR SHINING FACE,
WE'RE SO THRILLED YOU LIKE THE POOL,
BUT WHAT'S YOUR PLAN NOW, ACE?

I LIKE YOUR TIGER BOXERS,
I LIKE YOUR BASEBALL CAP,
I KNOW THIS IS A SHOCK, SIR:
GET A JOB AND CUT THE CRAP!

**CONGRATS ON GRADUATION.**
**YOU'VE NOW BECOME A MAN,**
**JUST ONCE RESIST TEMPTATION,**
**AND COME UP WITH A PLAN.**

YOUR INSTAGRAM IS AWESOME,
THOSE SNAPS ARE TRULY SICK,
REALLY!? ARE YOU SUCH A BUM?
GET A FUCKING JOB – AND QUICK!

YOU SAY YOU NEED A RECHARGE,
YOU SAY IT WILL BE FAST,
LIFE IS GOOD, LIVIN' LARGE!
DAMN! SIXTY DAYS HAVE PASSED!

YOUR FRIENDS ARE IN THE BASEMENT,
YOUR BEER IS ALL ON ICE,
PLEASE FIND SOME KIND OF PLACEMENT,
SOME DINEROS WOULD BE NICE!

SUCH AN ANGEL WHEN YOU NAP!
YOUR CHEEKS A ROSY PINK,
FUCKING A! YOU NEED A SLAP!
TAKE A SHOWER, DUDE, YOU STINK.

A HEDGE FUND WOULD BE GREAT, LOVE,
A START-UP WOULD BE SWELL,
TENDING BAR IS GOOD ENOUGH!
WHAT THE FUCK? OH, WHAT THE HELL.

I SEE YOU SEARCHING CRAIGSLIST,
IT SAYS THAT BOY SEEKS GIRL.
NEED YOU ASK WHY I'M SO PISSED?
THIS MAKES ME WANT TO HURL!

I LIKE THE WAY THAT SUIT FITS,
I DIG THE POCKET SQUARE.
COME BACK TO EARTH AND CUT THE SHIT;
WALL STREET'S GOT ENOUGH HOT AIR!

LA SUITS YOU TO A T,
NEW YORK WOULD BE ALL RIGHT,
NICE FANTASY, MS. FANCY-FREE!
JEEZ, GET A JOB – TONIGHT!

YOUR TAT'S A TRUE CREATION!
SO EDGY AND SO "ZEN,"
BUT SCREW THE MEDITATION!
YOU'LL GET A JOB? YEAH! WHEN!?

THE FALL'S ALMOST UPON US,
THE END OF SUMMER NIGH,
TELL ME, AND PLEASE BE HONEST:
WHY WON'T YOU FUCKING TRY?

BOOYAH! YOU ACED THE SCREEN TEST!
THEY'RE FILMING YOU AT SEA,
YOU'RE IN A DUMBASS CONTEST,
ON REALITY TV!

OUR HOUSE NOW BASKS IN SILENCE,
GONE IS OUR SURLY SLOB,
NO THREATS, NO TEARS, NO VIOLENCE,
YOU'VE FOUND A FUCKING "JOB."

CRAP! YOUR SHOW IS OVER,
TOO BAD THAT JACKASS WON,
BUT YOU'RE STILL IN THE CLOVER,
YOU'VE GOT YOUR ROOM BACK, HUN.

PHOTO CREDIT: ANTON PAPICH AND JEFF PREHN

ELISE HOFFMANN AND CHRIS NIEMCZEWSKI ARE INVESTMENT PROFESSIONALS IN WASHINGTON, D.C. THEY HAVE FOUR (ADULT) CHILDREN.

PHOTO CREDIT: JEFF PREHN

PHOTO CREDIT: ANTON PAPICH

ANTON PAPICH AND JEFF PREHN ARE LONGTIME PHOTOGRAPHY COLLABORATORS. ANTON LIVES IN WASHINGTON, D.C. AND JEFF LIVES IN NEW YORK CITY.

www.ingramcontent.com/pod-product-compliance
Lightning Source LLC
Chambersburg PA
CBHW041442010526
44118CB00003B/149